759 R

Modern Art

PAULINE RIDLEY

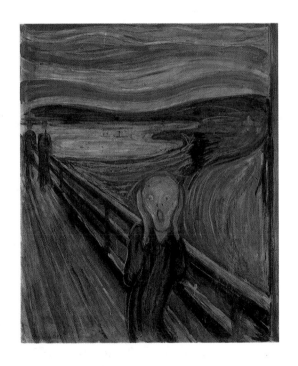

Wayland

ART AND ARTISTS

Ancient Art
Art in the Nineteenth Century
Impressionism
Modern Art
Renaissance Art
Western Art 1600-1800

Cover *Moon Woman* by Jackson Pollock. (Museum of Modern Art, New York.)

Title page *The Scream* by Edvard Munch. (National Gallery of Norway, Oslo.)

Picture editor: Shelley Noronha
Series and book editor: Rosemary Ashley
Designer: Simon Borrough

First published in 1995 by
Wayland (Publishers) Limited
61 Western Road
Hove
East Sussex, BN3 1JD, England

British Library Cataloguing in Publication Data
Ridley, Pauline
    Modern Art. – (Art & Artists Series)
    I. Title   II. Series
    709.04

    ISBN 0-7502-0978-X

Typeset by Dorchester Typesetting Group Limited
Printed and bound by L.E.G.O. S.p.A., Vicenza, Italy

Picture acknowledgements
The photographs in this book were supplied by: AKG London 8 (left), 11, 16, 29 (right), 39 (left); Bridgeman Art Library cover (main and background pictures), 5, 6, 7, 8 (right), 9 (right) 14, 15 (left), 17 (right), 18, 19 (both), 20, 21, (right), 23, 24, 25 (left), 27, 28, 30, 31, 32–3, 34 (both), 35, 37, 40, 41 (left); British Museum 10; Christies Colour Library 21 (left), 22; Eye Ubiquitous 4; E.T. Archive 26; Heydt Museum 13; National Gallery, Oslo 9 (left); Tate Gallery (London) 15 (right), 41 (right), 43 (right), 45 left); Tate Gallery (Liverpool) 45 (right); Topham Picture Library 39 (right); Visual Arts Library 12, 17 (left), 25 (right), 36, 44; Waddington Gallery 38; Women's Slide Library 29 (left). The photographs of works on pages 42 and 43 (left) were kindly supplied by the artists.

The following works are reproduced by permission of the copyright holders: © ADAGP, Paris and DACS, London 1995:– Constantin Brancusi *Sleeping Muse* (1910) p.17, Georges Braque *Clarinet and Bottle of Rum* (1911) p.15, Robert Delaunay *Homage to Blériot* (1914) p.17, Sonia Delaunay *Design for Clothes and Citroën* (1925) p.25, André Derain *Charing Cross Bridge* (1906) p.8, Marcel Duchamp *Bride Stripped Bare by her Bachelors. Even* (1923) p.19, Alberto Giacometti *Painted Bronze* (1950) p.36, Natalia Gontcharova *Le Coq d'Or* (1914) p.20, Arshile Gorky *The Waterfall* (1943) p.34, Wassily Kandinsky *Cossacks* (1910) p.12, René Magritte *The Human Condition II* (1935) p.29, Joan Miró *Head of Catalan Peasant* (1925) p.26; © ARS, NY and DACS, London 1995: – Willem de Kooning *Woman I* (1952) p.35, Mark Rothko *Red on Maroon* (1959) p.37, Frank Stella *Hyena Stomp* (1962) p.41; © DACS, London 1995:– Jean Arp *The Forest* (1916) p.19, Giorgio de Chirico *Italian Piazza: Melancholy* (1912) p.28, Fernand Léger *The Mechanic* (1920) p.23, Jules Grun *Friday at the French Artist's Salon* (1911) p.6, Hannah Höch *Priestess* (1934) p.22, Paul Klee *They're Biting* (1920) p.25, Meret Oppenheim *Fur Breakfast* (1936) p.29, Pablo Picasso *Les Demoiselles d'Avignon* (1907) p.14, *Still Life* (1914) p.15, *Guernica* (1937) pp. 32–3, Paul Signac *St Tropez* (1905) p.5; © David Smith/DACS, London/VAGA, New York 1995 David Smith *Cubi XVIII* (1964) p.40; Robert Rauschenberg/DACS, London/VAGA, New York 1995 Robert Rauschenberg *Retroactive II* (1964) p.39; © 1995 ABC/Mondrian Estate/Holtzman Trust. by ILP – Piet Mondrian *Composition with Red, Yellow and Blue* (1937) p.24; © Succession H. Matisse/DACS 1995 *Open Window, Collioure* (1905) p.7, *Goldfish* (1911) p.8.

Copyright permission has been sought for all works still in copyright, but in some instances it has been unobtainable. The publishers apologise for any omissions.

CONTENTS

1 INTRODUCTION

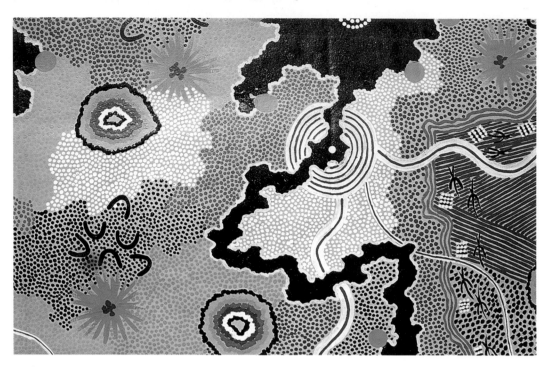

Mythological illustration by Michael Tommy Tjarbarudi. People often ask what modern art means, as though there was a secret code to help you read a hidden message. But the meaning of all kinds of art changes in different situations. For instance, the patterns in Australian Aboriginal bark paintings originally symbolized a sacred connection between people and land; now they are found on T-shirts promoting the tourist industry, or hung in art galleries like abstract paintings. But these works can also help to teach people something about their makers' lives and beliefs. When young Aboriginal Australian artists use these dot patterns today, they are drawing on *all* those meanings to explore their heritage and their place in modern Australia.

Some of the work discussed in this book was made before your great-grandparents were born. So why is it still called 'modern' art? Cars and planes made at the same time seem very old-fashioned now, because we expect them to change. But people sometimes assume that art should always stay the same, describing the world in the same ways.

If you look at other books in this series, you will see that the word 'art' is used to describe many different types of object – masks and pots, paintings and statues. They have different jobs to do, such as decorating people's homes, telling stories, recording the appearance of people and places, and playing a part in religious ceremonies.

In the fifteenth century, artists developed new ways of representing the appearance of the world to help them to tell religious stories as vividly as possible. The same techniques were used to record what people looked like, but the invention of photography in the nineteenth century made this less important. By then, everyday life was changing. More people lived in cities, and new technology was speeding up travel and communication. Each generation was very conscious that modern life was different from their parents' experience.

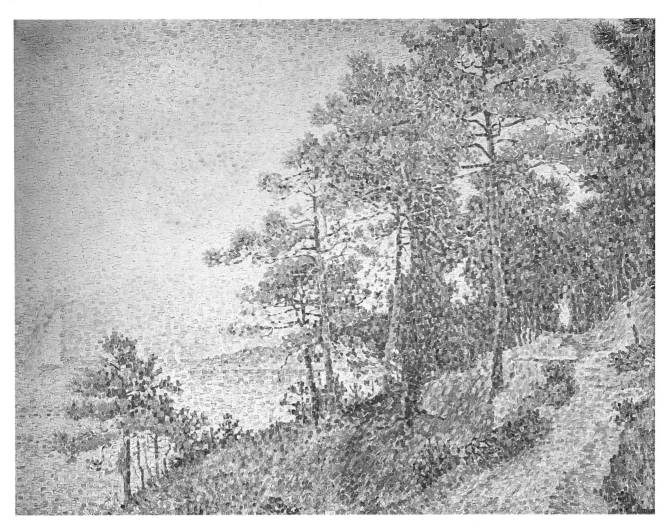

St Tropez by Paul Signac (1863–1935). These dots have a different purpose from the pattern in the bark painting opposite. They reflect an interest in scientific colour theory as well as the surface pattern of a painting. Work such as this bridged Impressionist art and Matisse's early work. (Musée des Beaux Arts, Grenoble.)

Some people wanted art to show those changes; others preferred to stick to familiar ways of seeing the world. Later in this book you will see that arguments about what art should look like are usually connected to disagreements about what it is for.

Traditional 'realistic' painting was a skill which almost anyone could be taught but, now that very few of us learn it, it can seem like magic. Many people still feel annoyed or disappointed by anything that seems different, especially art that is completely abstract – that is, it doesn't try to copy the appearance of the world around us.

Liking classical music, however, does not stop us from enjoying jazz or rock, and it would be a shame to let admiration for traditional skills make us close our eyes and minds to other forms of visual expression. Painting and sculpture (and all kinds of video and performance art that cannot really be shown in books) can deal with ideas and feelings which are impossible to express in words or music. When we are born, seeing and touching are our most important senses for finding out about the world. Throughout our lives we are surrounded by images that can affect the way we feel about ourselves. Art can help us to explore this part of our lives.

2 THE ART WORLD – MATISSE AND FAUVISM

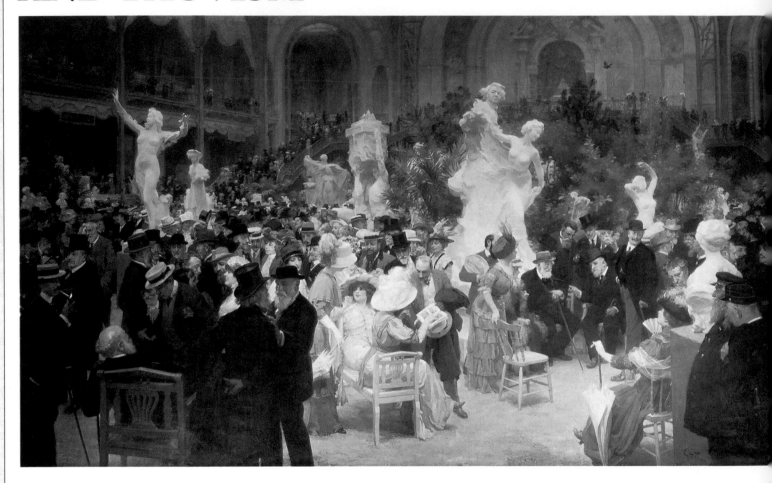

In the past, artists earned their living by making paintings and sculptures to order, for people who wanted them. By the beginning of the twentieth century, however, most artists worked without a particular customer in mind. They would try to get their work shown at one of the big art exhibitions that were held every year. They hoped to attract the attention of the art critics who wrote for the newspapers, trusting that this publicity would encourage someone to buy. It was like the music industry today, where groups usually have to get signed up by a record company, then get their record played and talked about on the radio before people will go and buy it.

At this time, artists and critics were beginning to talk less about what was pictured in a painting (its subject) and much more about how it was painted. Let's think about what that means.

You have probably discovered for yourself that if you draw a small tree next to a big one, the small one will seem further away. A more complete version of this technique was worked out in the fifteenth century. It was called 'perspective' (which means 'seeing through') and was used to make a flat surface look as though you could see through it, like a window, to a real scene on the other side.

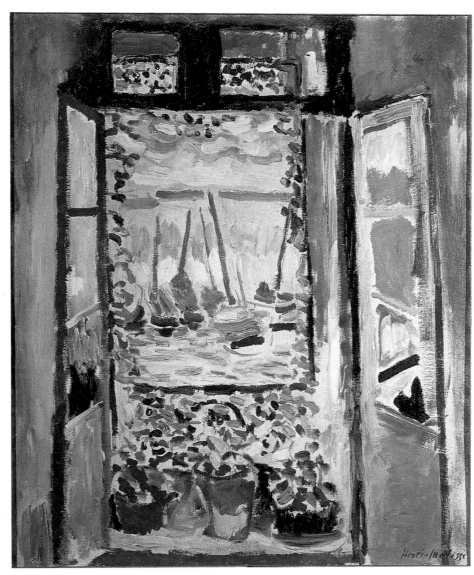

Left *Open Window, Collioure* by Henri Matisse. This is a tiny picture compared to the painting opposite, but the use of colour gives it lots of energy. The boats in the harbour seem just as near as the flowerpots on the balcony, because of the way the reds and greens sizzle, pulling our eyes back to the painted surface of the picture. (John Hay Whitney Collection, New York.)

Far left *Friday at the Salon* by Jules Grun (1868–1934). The fashionable crowds at the official Salon seem more interested in each other than in the work on display. Many younger artists preferred to show their work at smaller independent Salons, where it could have more impact. (Musée des Beaux Arts, Rouen.)

'Isms' and Insults

Music journalists and disc jockeys often use general labels like 'heavy metal' or 'house music' to describe different types of sound. In the same way, critics trying to pick out new tendencies in art would often invent labels like 'Impressionism' or 'Cubism'. Sometimes, a group might invent its own name, especially if the members wanted to get some publicity, but many names started as insults in the popular press, such as when Matisse and his friends were called 'fauves' (wild beasts) when they showed their work.

When you look through a real window, you usually notice only what is on the other side, not the glass itself. With traditional painting the same is true. We do not notice the painting so much as what is in the picture.

By the early years of the twentieth century, following the example of the Impressionists and the later work, sometimes called 'Post-Impressionist', of Paul Cézanne (1839–1906), Georges Seurat (1859–91) and Paul Gauguin (1849–1903) many younger artists were interested in exploring a looser style, using paint in a more obvious way and with more adventurous use of colour.

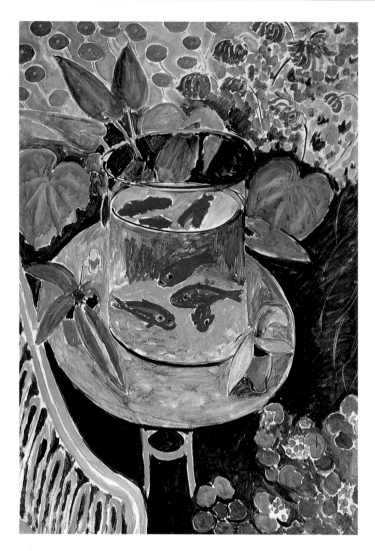

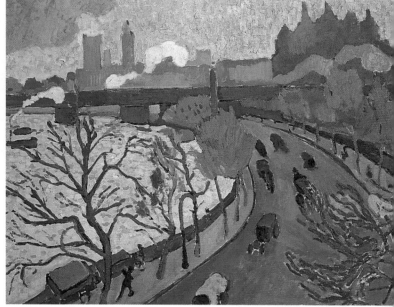

Left *The Goldfish Bowl* by Henri Matisse. Greens contrast vibrantly with pinks and oranges while the black helps to sharpen the design. The thinly applied paint looks casual, but the picture is carefully observed – see how the light refracts the image of the goldfish on the water surface. (Pushkin Museum, Moscow.)

Above *Charing Cross Bridge* by André Derain, who made several paintings of the Thames during a visit to London. (Tate Gallery, London.)

When Henri Matisse (1869–1954) was painting in the south of France, he found that bright sunshine tends to make colours look pale. But, if you paint them like that, you lose the feeling of heat and light. One solution Matisse and his friends discovered was to use large patches of pure, bright colour with a lot of white between them. They also found that, as the patches became larger, the pattern they made on the surface became as important as the subject of the picture.

When Matisse, along with Maurice de Vlaminck (1876–1958) and André Derain (1880–1954), showed this kind of work at the Autumn Salon in Paris in 1905, the critics called them 'fauves', or 'wild beasts'. But Matisse was not just trying to be shocking. In fact he later said that he wanted his art to be like a comforting armchair that you could rest in. Some people have argued that art should be more than simply beautiful decoration for the walls of people rich enough to buy it. They believe that art should be uncomfortable because it should make us ask questions about how we see things or about social issues. Matisse, however, who had originally started painting when he was ill, believed that we all need art to make us feel better – simple, peaceful images that raise our spirits.

3 EXPRESSIONISM

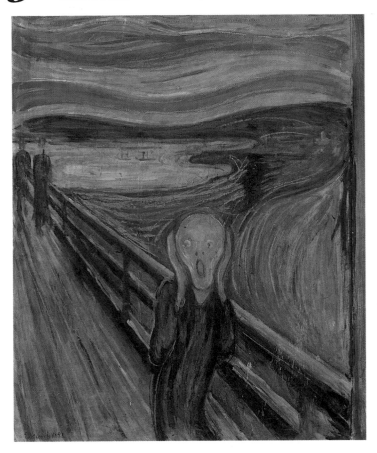

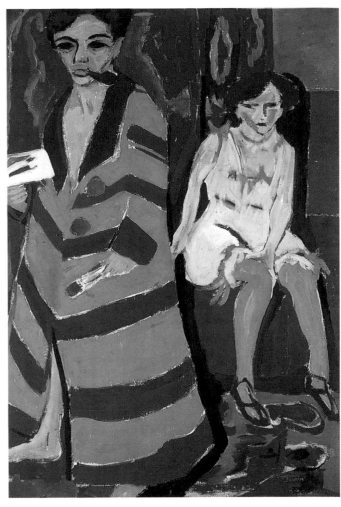

Above *The Scream* by Edvard Munch (1863–1944). (National Gallery of Norway, Oslo.)

Right *Self-portrait with Model* by Ernst Ludwig Kirchner. (Kunsthalle, Hamburg.)

While Matisse wanted his pictures to be joyful, many of the Scandinavian and German artists known as Expressionists were more interested in violent or unhappy feelings. They painted a great many self-portraits, staring into the mirror, and out of the picture, trying to explore their most extreme states of mind.

In earlier times nobody would have been interested in what artists were feeling. They were just expected to use their skills to do their job. But, during the nineteenth century, people began to think of artists (and poets and composers) as especially sensitive, able to express stronger feelings than other people.

In Germany, a number of artists formed a group known as Die Brücke (The Bridge). They included Ernst Ludwig Kirchner (1880–1938), Erich Heckel (1883–1970) and Karl Schmidt-Rottluff (1884–1976). They valued truthfulness more than clever techniques, and in fact, they often used deliberately rough ways of working as if that was a proof of the strength of their feelings. Their interest in simple, direct expression made them enthusiastic about the kind of art they called 'primitive'. This included work from almost every society outside Europe as well as peasant art from their own countries, although it was African art that had the most influence on them.

Primitivism

'Primitive' originally just meant 'from early times'. When European explorers began to travel round the world in the fifteenth and sixteenth centuries, they found countries with cultures different from their own. They decided they must be less developed, even when these cultures were thousands of years old. When the Europeans wanted to take the resources of these countries, they claimed that they were bringing progress. Objects from these countries, however beautifully made, were brought back to Europe as curiosities and put in museums to show how 'savage' their makers were. At the beginning of the twentieth century, some European artists came to admire and copy the style of these curiosities. This is sometimes referred to as 'Primitivism' but the word is also used to describe a general preference for simplicity, in any period.

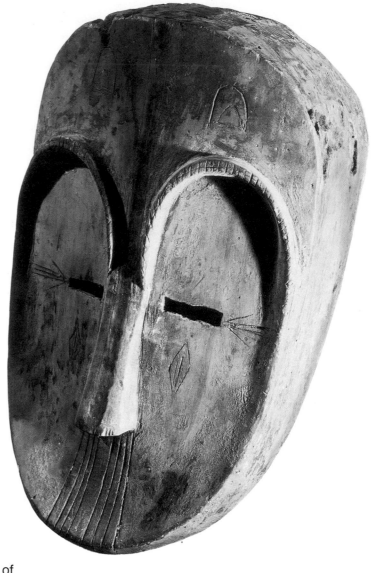

Right A Bakongo tribal mask from Africa. Masks like this, which seemed to possess a ritual power because of their use in religious ceremonies, fascinated many artists at the beginning of the twentieth century, including Pablo Picasso (see page 14).

By 1900, some people were beginning to believe that modern civilization had become too artificial and that human beings, crowded into cities, had lost touch with their true nature. From this point of view, societies that appeared to be simpler looked more attractive. The strange objects in museums, such as tribal masks and carved figures, seemed mysterious and exciting to artists who wanted to make powerfully expressive art themselves. Knowing very little about the people who had made these things, or what they were for, made it easier for the European artists to imagine whatever suited their own ideas.

Little children who are frightened by their own anger often imagine 'scary monsters'. Adults also sometimes deal with complicated feelings by imagining they belong to someone or some place outside themselves. Many of the Expressionist artists were unhappy and confused. The idea of the 'primitive' gave them

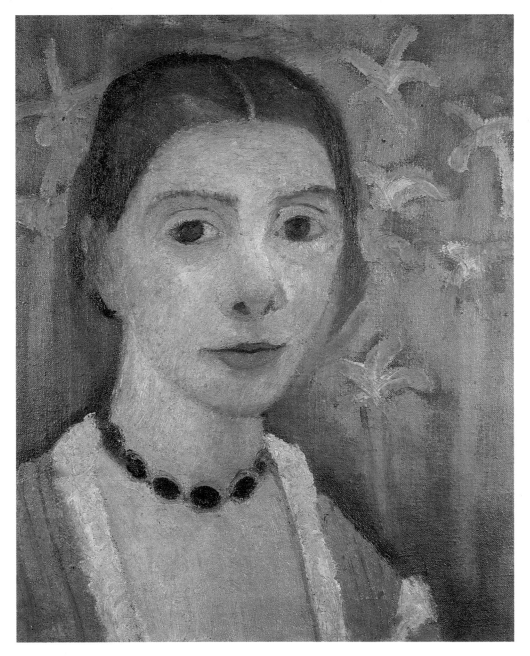

Self-portrait with Irises by Paula Modersohn-Becker. This serious, self-questioning image contrasts with Kirchner's spiky self-portrait on page 9. Disturbed by women's new independence, many male artists in the early 1900s portrayed themselves as powerful, even brutal figures. Women artists had to overcome the myth of the 'macho' genius. (Private collection.)

a safe place to explore these strong feelings away from the realities of modern life.

At the end of the nineteenth century a similar impulse had led Paul Gauguin to leave France and go to work in Tahiti and the Marquesas Islands, in the Pacific. Many of the Expressionists admired Gauguin's work, and because they usually lived in cities, they were attracted by the idea of going back to nature, to the 'other' world of peasant life in the country.

In the same way, because most of them were men, Expressionist artists saw women as 'the Other'. Many of their pictures show women as mysterious creatures, sometimes weak, sometimes threatening, but always less civilized and closer to nature than men. Of course, these images had nothing to do with real women. Many women artists of the time, like Paula Modersohn-Becker (1876–1907), struggled to resolve the contradictions between their own lives and ideas they shared with Expressionism.

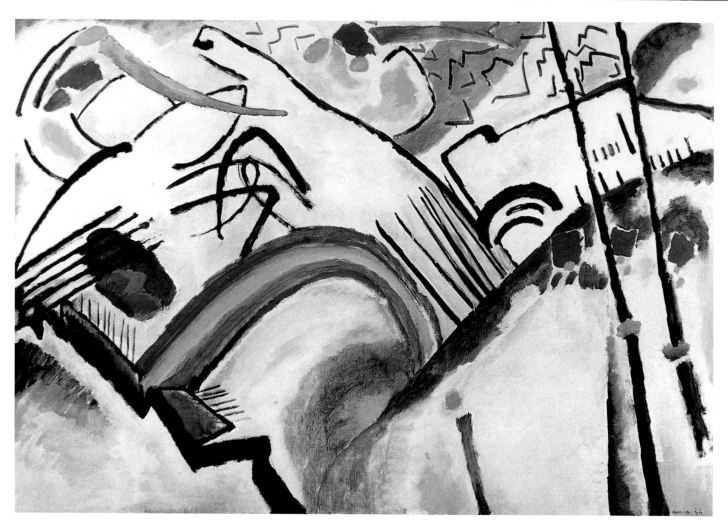

Composition by Wassily Kandinsky. Musical titles encourage us to think about the general mood the painter is trying to create. But the picture's other title – *Cossacks* – might prompt us to find the soldiers on the right-hand side. Can you make them out, with their red hats and long bayonets, and does this change the way you look at the painting? (Tate Gallery, London.)

The search for more powerful means of expression went deeper than simply borrowing primitive subjects and techniques. Towards the end of the nineteenth century, Gauguin and the Symbolists had already begun to explore how a picture could create mood through the use of colours and shapes rather than through what people thought about the subject.

There was a lot of discussion about whether painting should stop imitating the appearance

of things and become more like music. Music does not usually copy anything but it can still make us feel very strongly – happy or sad, excited or peaceful.

Wassily Kandinsky (1866–1944), a Russian artist who came to work in Germany, used the bright colours and patterns of Russian folk art in his early work. He was especially interested in the connection between music and pictures because he often 'saw' certain colours in his

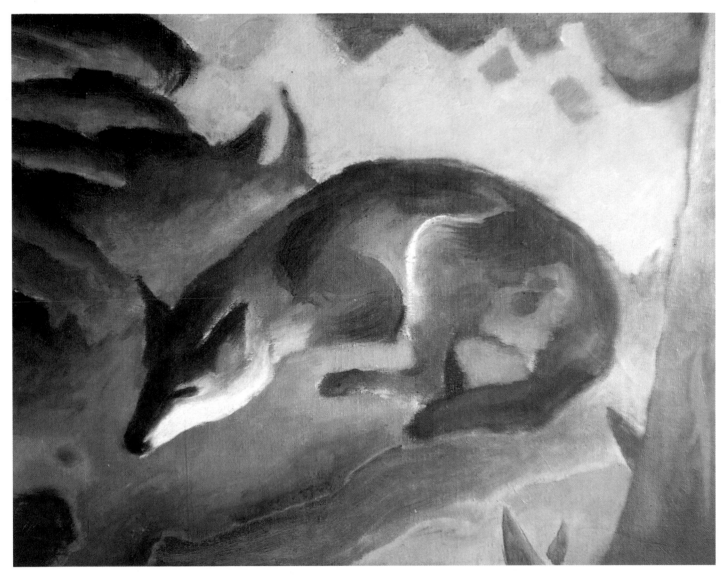

The Purple Fox by Franz Marc. Marc thought animals were nobler than humans, and he tried to imagine how nature would seem through the eyes of an eagle or a dog. He believed colours had symbolic meanings: blue was spiritual; red, heavy and brutal; yellow, gentle and cheerful. (Heydr Museum, Wuppertal, Germany.)

head when he heard particular sounds. He also said that he could 'hear' colours. This may seem an odd thing to suggest, but we quite often use words which describe sounds to say something about what we see – we talk, for example, of 'loud' colours or colours which 'clash'.

In 1911, Kandinsky and Franz Marc (1880–1916) founded a group called Der Blaue Reiter (Blue Rider). They published a book showing work by modern artists alongside primitive and folk art and children's drawings. Kandinsky believed that art should be about spiritual beliefs rather than surface appearances. Catching sight of one of his pictures lying upside down in the half light one evening convinced him that the abstract qualities of a painting were more important than the subject. For a few more years, however, Kandinsky still used the outer world as a starting point for his paintings.

4 CUBISM AND AFTER

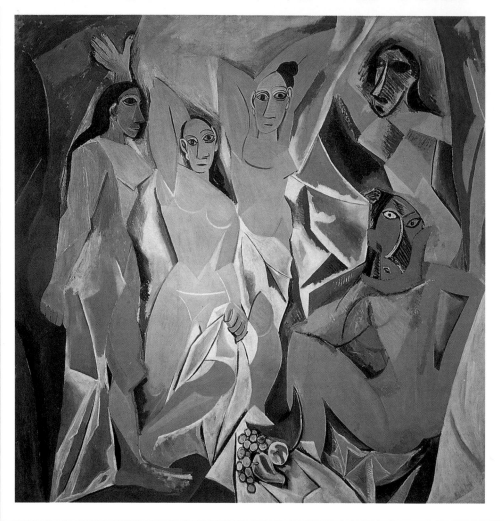

Left *Les Demoiselles d'Avignon (The Girls of Avignon Street)* by Pablo Picasso. This painting made people question the 'pin-up' poses found in Academic paintings of nude women, by giving them faces borrowed from Iberian sculpture and African masks, similar to the one on page 10. (Museum of Modern Art, New York.)

Right *Still Life with Fringing* by Picasso. The artist has played sophisticated games with space in this apparently simple construction. The wooden 'glass' is hollow but its open end is solid and casts a real shadow, while the shadows on the mouldings are painted. The fringe is a joke about gold frames on Old Master paintings. (Tate Gallery, London.)

When Pablo Picasso (1881–1973) first showed *Les Demoiselles d'Avignon* to his friends in 1907, they hated it. The big ugly painting, with its cartoon-like faces, seemed to be deliberately making fun of everything they admired, including Picasso's own earlier work – gentle, rather sad pictures of circus people and beggars.

Even today, after nearly ninety years, this is still a shocking picture. The life-size figures, with their awkward bodies, glare down at you blankly. You may have guessed from the two faces on the right that Picasso, like the Expressionists, was impressed by African masks, which did play a very big part in the development of this picture. But the reason that this painting came to seem so important to the history of modern art was because of the way Picasso treated space.

Space in pictures is hard to talk about because, of course, it's not really there – it is just an illusion. It can be useful to imagine making a three-dimensional model of what you see in the picture. A traditional type of painting would be rather like a model theatre, with figures standing firmly on the floor, some of them close to the front of the stage while others may be towards the back. For the Picasso painting,

Right *Clarinet and Bottle of Rum on a Mantelpiece* by Georges Braque. The fireplace at the bottom of the picture has a marble scroll supporting the mantelpiece. Everything seems to tilt in different directions. Can you find the clarinet behind the bottle, and the nail with its painted shadow? (Tate Gallery, London.)

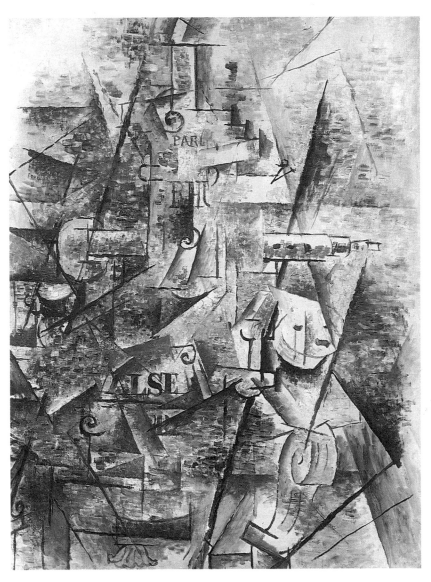

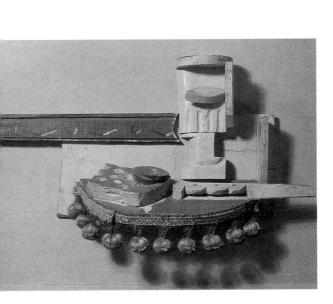

to make a three-dimensional model you would need to cut the figures out of cardboard and push them up against the front, with the space between them taken up with something like crumpled paper. Just trying to work out which parts of the picture are in front of which shows how difficult it would be.

The pictures that Picasso and his friend Georges Braque (1882–1963) painted between 1907 and 1912 were called Cubist, because a critic said that some of them looked as if they were made of little cubes. Some of the earliest ones were rocky landscapes but, later, Picasso and Braque tended to concentrate on their everyday surroundings, depicting objects in cafés or studios.

You will sometimes hear it said that Cubist paintings show objects from several sides, but the effect is more like looking through a kaleidoscope, which breaks up the image into little bits. Imagine you are drawing a still-life. Instead of standing back to get an overall view, imagine that you get in close and draw each part almost as if you were touching it. These separate fragments won't necessarily join up in the imaginary space of the picture, but they could come together as a pattern of brushmarks on the surface.

Collage

The name comes from the French word, *coller*, meaning to stick. Sticking paper or other materials on to a flat surface to help make a picture is such a simple technique that it is astonishing to realize how important it has been for the development of twentieth-century art. Cutting and sticking coloured paper helped artists to think of pictures as arrangements of flat shapes. Images and photographs could also be put together to make political comments (see photomontage on page 22) or odd dream-like combinations (see pictures on pages 26–9). Transferred to three dimensions, collage also introduced the possibility of constructed sculpture (see Picasso's construction on page 15). Today collage is widely used in advertising and illustration.

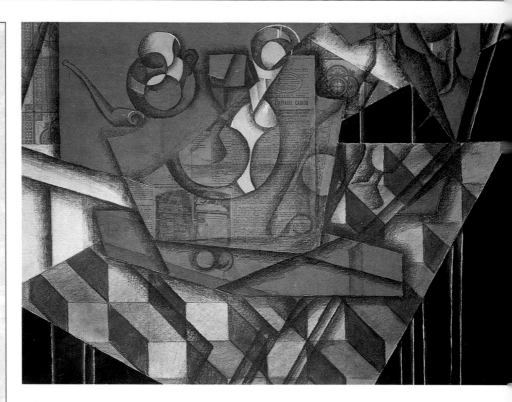

Teacups by Juan Gris. Shading confuses the difference between flat pattern and illusions of depth. Gris has also included a private joke about Cubism – a newspaper story about a new law banning poster-sticking ('collage') on public monuments. (Kunstslig, Dusseldorf.)

Picasso and Braque stopped using bright colour for a while because they wanted to concentrate on drawing. It is important to remember that they were not trying to make abstract paintings but wanted to find new ways of drawing objects in space. To make sure that the subject did not disappear completely from their pictures, they would put in little 'clues' – more carefully painted details like violin strings or buttons or letters. (You can unscramble most Cubist paintings by using the title to help you look for these clues.) At this time they were not showing their work at the Salons but were painting just for themselves and a few other people, so it did not matter if their pictures were hard to understand.

After a while, Picasso and Braque began to think that it would make sense to replace the details with the real thing. What was the point of carefully painting a copy of the label on a bottle when you could stick the label straight on to the picture? They liked this reminder that pictures are real, solid objects, just like anything else in the world. They began to use pieces of newspaper, chopping headlines to make jokes and puns, and mixing news items into pictures of their everyday surroundings. This technique, developed in 1912, was known as 'collage' and was quickly taken up by the third major Cubist painter, Juan Gris (1887–1927).

Once you begin sticking things on to a picture, it is quite a small step to make thicker, more three-dimensional constructions. Picasso started to construct small models of the guitars and wineglasses he featured in his paintings,

Right *Homage to Blériot* by Robert Delaunay. This painting celebrated the first aeroplane flight over the English Channel. Can you find the Eiffel Tower and the plane's propellor? (Musée d'Art Moderne, Paris.)

Below *Sleeping Muse* by Constantin Brancusi. The first version of this was carved in marble, the features barely breaking the hard surface. Here it is cast in bronze and polished to a smooth sheen. (Metropolitan Museum of Art, New York.)

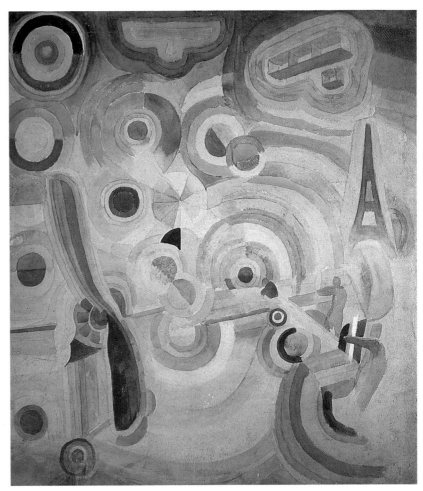

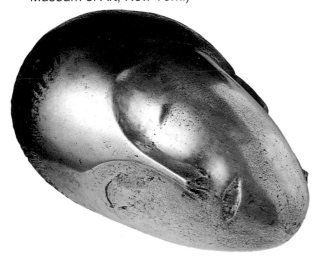

first from folded paper and card, and later in metal or wood. He probably did not think of them as 'sculpture' at first. Sculpture had traditionally been made by modelling a figure (usually in clay, which would then be cast in metal), or carving (into stone or wood).

Auguste Rodin (1840–1917) had already begun to change the first method from something suitable for monumental statues of important people to a much more lively and experimental medium. Constantin Brancusi (1876–1957), who had arrived in Paris in 1904, was beginning to explore the medium of carved and polished marble, alongside the rich woodcarving tradition of his native Romania. Now, Cubist 'constructions' suggested a third and extremely productive way of thinking about what sculpture could be.

Many artists passed through a Cubist phase before moving on in different directions. Unlike some of the artists in the last chapter, many found life in a modern city like Paris very exciting. They enjoyed the crowds and cars, the babble of information from posters, newspapers and conversations overheard in the street. The broken-up quality of Cubist painting and collage seemed a good way to show all this excitement in pictures.

A group of Italian artists, calling themselves Futurists, celebrated modern machines and the speed of planes and racing cars. Robert Delaunay (1885–1941) and his wife Sonia (1884–1979) (see page 25) painted scenes of Paris and the effects of light, using bright colours like those in the work of Matisse and Kandinsky.

5 ARTISTS AND THE WAR

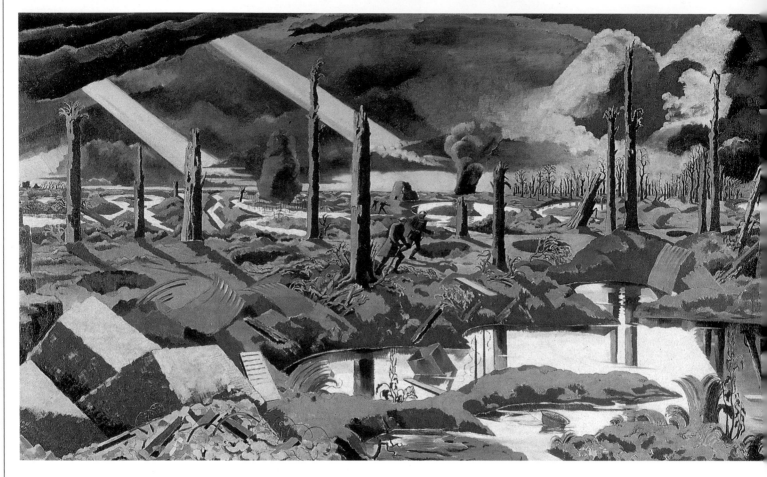

The Menin Road by Paul Nash. The jagged pattern of lines increases the effect of this nightmare landscape of mud and rubble, the result of four years of trench warfare during the First World War. (Imperial War Museum, London.)

Many of the newspapers used in the Cubist collages of 1912 refer to fighting in eastern Europe, which a lot of people were worried about at that time. By 1914, this conflict had developed into something much bigger – the First World War, which continued until 1918. The effects of the war were enormous. So many soldiers were killed or injured that it seemed as though a whole generation of young men had been destroyed. The war also destroyed people's confidence in ideas of progress. Scientific invention, instead of helping people, was being used to make more effective weapons. Although soldiers on both sides started out believing they were fighting

for a good cause, by 1916 many felt that the politicians and the generals were carrying on the war pointlessly.

Some artists tried to show people back home what the battlefields were really like. Others tried to avoid the war altogether. A small group of artists from several different countries ended up in Zurich in Switzerland, which was not involved in the conflict.

In 1916, the group started a combined club and art gallery called the Cabaret Voltaire. The name they chose for their activities was Dada – a nonsense word, a child's first sounds. If the

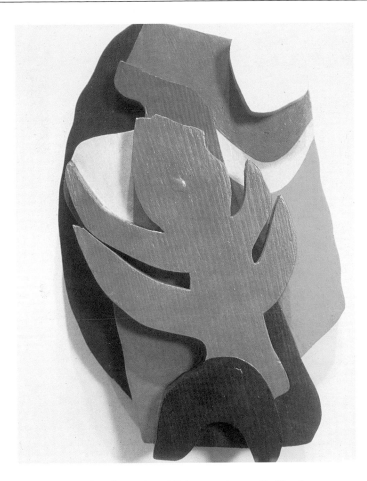

The Forest by Jean Arp. This wooden relief looks simple, almost innocent, as if Arp was deliberately avoiding the world of war and machines. (National Gallery of Art, Washington.)

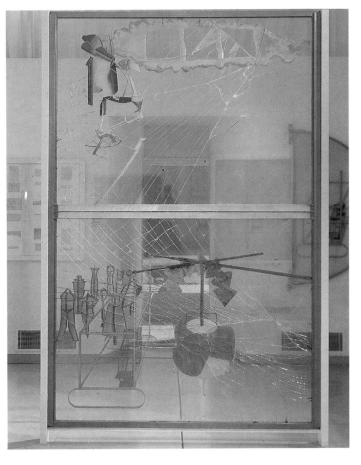

The Bride Stripped Bare by her Bachelors. Even (The Large Glass) by Marcel Duchamp. This elaborate, unfinished story of a 'mechanical' bride was smashed on its way to an exhibition. Duchamp spent months piecing it together, pleased that an accident had finally completed the work. (Philadelphia Museum of Art.)

supposedly sensible, adult world had led to the madness of war, then they didn't want to belong to it.

They also wanted to avoid making the kind of art that would end up in museums or on the walls of houses of the rich people who they blamed for the war. So they made masks and puppets and, like the Futurists had done, performed noise music and nonsense poetry. The Alsace-born artist Jean Arp (1887–1966) wrote later, 'While the thunder of the guns rumbled in the distance, we pasted, we recited . . . we sang with all our soul . . . (to) save mankind from the madness of those times.'

In New York, the name Dada was adopted by another group of artists, including the Frenchmen Marcel Duchamp (1887–1968) and Francis Picabia (1879–1953), and the American Man Ray (1890–1977). They were less concerned about the war and society, but used humour to question traditional ideas about art. Marcel Duchamp took ordinary objects, slightly altered or given a title, and exhibited them as 'ready-mades'. He was not claiming that these objects were particularly beautiful – in fact he deliberately tried to avoid letting his taste affect his choice – but he wanted people to think about the assumptions we make when we decide whether something is art or not.

6 THE RUSSIAN REVOLUTION – ART AND POLITICS

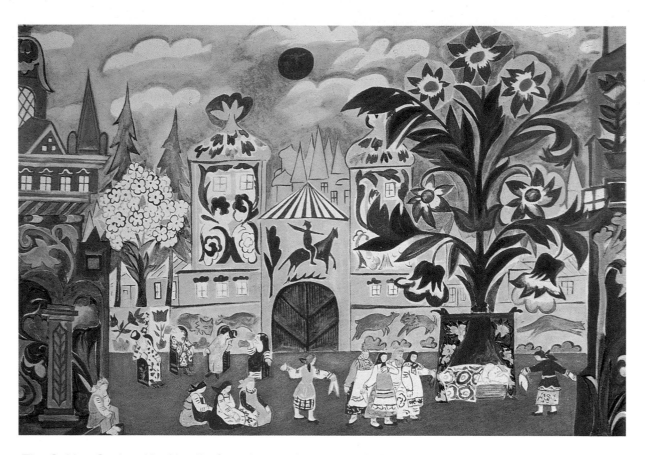

The Golden Cockerel by Natalia Gontcharova (1881–1962). This stage design for the Russian Ballet, mixes folk art and Cubism. (Private collection.)

Before the First World War, artists of all nationalities came to work in the major European cities. Magazines and exhibitions of modern art spread the new ideas from one country to another. Russia was part of this international movement. Some Russian artists, like Kandinsky, went to work abroad, while rich merchants in Moscow and St Petersburg were important early collectors of work by Picasso and Matisse.

At the time, there was a revival of interest in traditional Russian folk art. For foreigners this was just another kind of exotic, primitive art.

The Russian Ballet, for example, had a big success in Paris with works like Stravinsky's *The Firebird* and *Petrushka*. But for Russian artists, peasant art was also a way of rediscovering a sense of national identity and pride. (Similar feelings were emerging all over Europe. Nationalism could be a source of pride – but it also helped to cause the First World War.)

In his early work, Kasimir Malevich (1878–1935) combined these Russian themes with a form of Cubism. But unlike the Cubists, and like Kandinsky (see page 12), he believed that art should express the invisible, spiritual

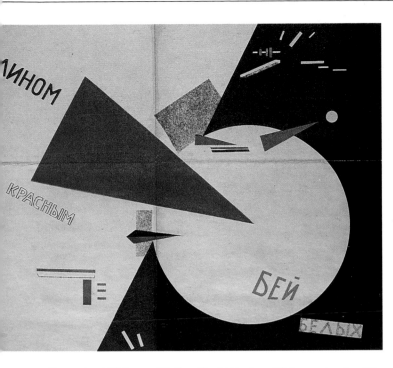

Beat the Whites with the Red Wedge. This poster by El Lissitsky (1890–1941) describes the struggle between Red (Revolutionary) forces and White (Tsarist) forces. Magazines today still show the influence of the Russian's use of bold colours and lettering. (Private collection.)

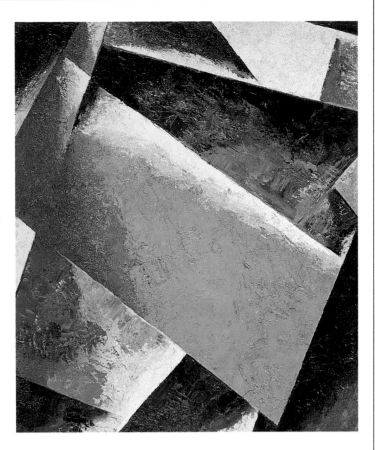

Architectonic Composition by Liubov Popova. This energetic work seems to reflect the excitement felt by many about the Russian Revolution. (Leonard Hutton Galleries, New York.)

world and that it could not do that if it was tied to the real world. In 1915, he exhibited his first completely abstract painting, a black square on a white background. It was hung across the corner of the room, the traditional place for Russian icons (religious paintings).

When the Russian Revolution swept away the old rule of the Tsars in 1917, the younger artists were enthusiastic. They wanted to help build the new society in which everybody would be equal. Most of them agreed that the visual language that was appropriate to this new world was not the traditional art of the academies but the new abstract art, with simple geometric shapes which everyone could understand. Over the next few years, while Russia struggled through civil war, food shortages and foreign invasion, some people came to believe that art should have a practical use. Vladimir Tatlin (1885–1953), Liubov Popova (1889–1924) and Varvara Stepanova (1894–1958), among others, wanted to be more like engineers than artists, using their knowledge of materials, their visual skills and inventiveness to design industrial goods and posters, books and textiles, which would be of immediate use in everyday life. Film and

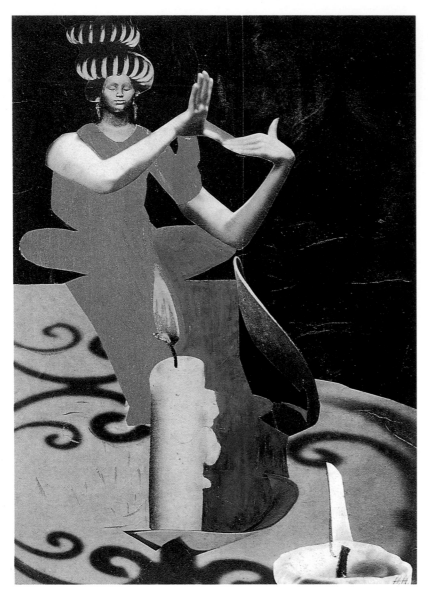

Priestess by Hannah Höch. Höch's Dada photomontages mixed politics with an interest in images of women. Here she has used contrasts of light and dark, sight and touch, and repeated curves and scrolls to make a gentle, sensuous image. (Private collection.)

Photomontage
This is a kind of collage made from photographs. Early in the twentieth century in Berlin, artists like Hannah Höch and Raoul Hausmann were bringing together separate images from newspapers, magazines and advertising to make jokes or comments on current events or politics. Because photography was associated with the everyday world, these images could have more impact than paintings, especially when they were re-photographed to appear more believable. Later, John Heartfield used this technique to campaign against the rise of Adolf Hitler and Fascism, and was eventually forced to leave Germany.

photography, because they represented technology and progress, were an important part of this new art known as Constructivism.

In Germany, another group of artists was enthusiastic about Constructivist ideas and also hoped to bring about political change. As the 1914–18 war came to an end, the defeated Germans were hungry and disillusioned. Some artists turned to Expressionism, with its stress on inner feelings, but this seemed like feeble escapism to Richard Huelsenbeck (1892–1974), who came back to Berlin in 1917 from Zurich full of excitement about the Dada events there.

He and his colleagues – who included George Grosz (1893–1959), John Heartfield (1891–1968), Raoul Hausmann (1886–1971) and Hannah Höch (1889–1978) – adopted the name Dada for their own movement. Dada in Berlin was more political than in other cities. Rather than making anti-art gestures to change the way people thought about art, the Berlin artists hoped to change society. George Grosz used his drawing skills to make savage caricatures of those people who had made a profit out of the war, but the most important medium of the Berlin Dada artists was photomontage (see above).

7 INTO THE TWENTIES – THE SEARCH FOR ORDER

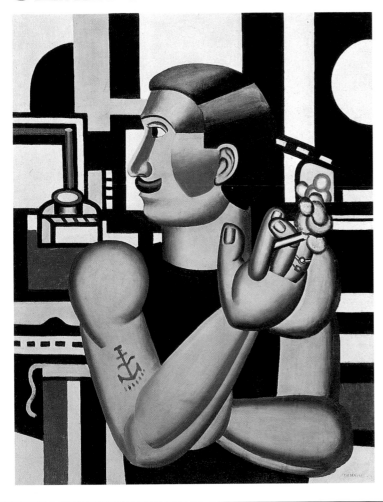

The Mechanic by Fernand Léger. Léger admired the precision of modern machines and the skill of the workers who made them. Here he combined a clean-cut mechanical style with the solemn profile found in Egyptian art to produce a heroic but down-to-earth image of a modern working man. (National Gallery of Canada, Ottawa.)

We have seen how some artists turned away from the traditional values of society and of the businessmen and politicians they blamed for the war. A different way to cope with the horror of what had happened was to look for comforting images of peace and stability.

In France, pictures of mothers and babies became popular for a while, and some artists turned back to traditional styles. But critics also began to point out that certain types of modern art had something in common with the solid, carefully composed works of seventeenth-century painters like Nicholas Poussin and Claude Lorraine. Looked at in this way, the work of Cézanne and later artists like Fernand Léger (1881–1955) could be seen to carry on the classical tradition in French art – solid geometric figures in calm, balanced compositions (see *The Mechanic* above).

Even completely abstract art could offer images of balance and order. The Dutch painter Piet Mondrian (1872–1944) shared with Kandinsky and Malevich the belief that art should deal with the spiritual side of life. His early work showed the Dutch landscape, with its flatness broken by the vertical lines of trees or

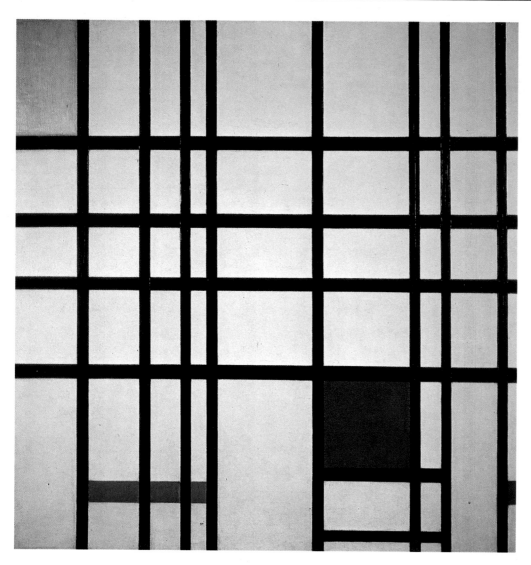

Composition by Piet Mondrian. From the mid 1920s, Mondrian used a limited range of colours and shapes. These patterns have come to stand for an idea of modernity, used in so many kinds of design that the hand-painted subtlety of the originals can come as a surprise. Look at the careful spacing of the lines and the effect of leaving the black edges off some of the coloured blocks. (Tate Gallery, London.)

windmills, using colour in a heightened, symbolic way. Around 1910 he discovered Cubism and for a while he worked in Paris, making a series of paintings which gradually simplified images of the real world into a pattern of straight lines. Back in Holland during the First World War, he continued this process with his series called *Pier and Ocean*.

Mondrian believed that reality is based on a series of opposites (similar to the Buddhist idea of yin and yang): horizontal and vertical, dark and light, female and male. He believed the artist could help people towards spiritual truth by offering images of perfect balance, which could never be achieved in the everyday world. Even people who disagree completely with his views can be moved by the care with which Mondrian pursued his ideal. Using only the primary colours (red, yellow and blue) along with black and white, he would paint and repaint each picture until the balance seemed exactly right.

A group of artists and designers associated with Mondrian in Holland were known by the name of the magazine they published, De Stijl (The Style). They used a similar range of clean, square shapes and primary colours, but were mainly interested in applying them to the design of architecture, furniture, magazines and posters.

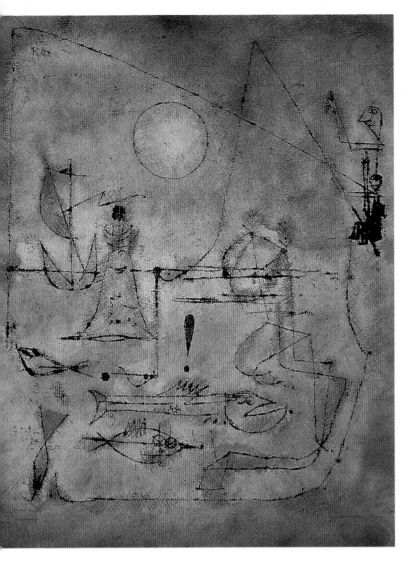

Left *They're Biting*, by Paul Klee. This tiny picture uses a combination of water colour and drawing, which Klee described as 'taking a line for a walk.' His ideas about art combined a poetic imagination with an interest in order and form. (Tate Gallery, London.)

Below *Coat and Citroën Car*. Sonia Delaunay designed these for the Paris Exhibition of Decorative Arts (Art Deco). They show how easily developments in painting, such as *Homage to Blériot* (page 17), were absorbed into other areas of design. (Bibliothéque Nationale, Paris.)

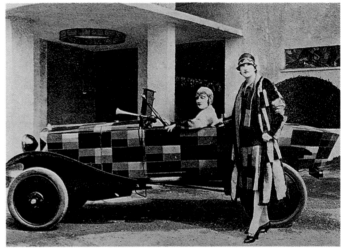

The ideas common to the De Stijl group and the Russian Constructivists were also encouraged by a new kind of art school, the Bauhaus, set up in Germany in 1919. Here, the search was for the most rational and functional architecture, design and craftsmanship. Students were taught to investigate the basic elements of form and colour by artists and designers from all over Europe, including Kandinsky, Paul Klee(1879–1940) and László Moholy-Nagy (1895–1946). In the practical workshops, they also learnt the use of different materials and were eventually encouraged to design for industrial production. When Hitler came to power in Germany in 1933, the Bauhaus was forced to close and many of the staff fled to England and the USA. Even today, the influence of the Bauhaus is still strong, in art education and in the design of many household objects.

All over Europe and the USA, similar work (known as the International Modern style) was based on a belief that buildings, furniture and domestic goods should be designed like cars or aeroplanes – to do their job as simply and effectively as possible, stripped of unnecessary ornament. This rational approach was displayed by the architect Le Corbusier (1888–1965) in his Pavilion of the New Spirit, designed for the 1925 International Exhibition of the Decorative Arts, and summed up in his statement, 'a house is a machine for living in'.

8 SURREALISM

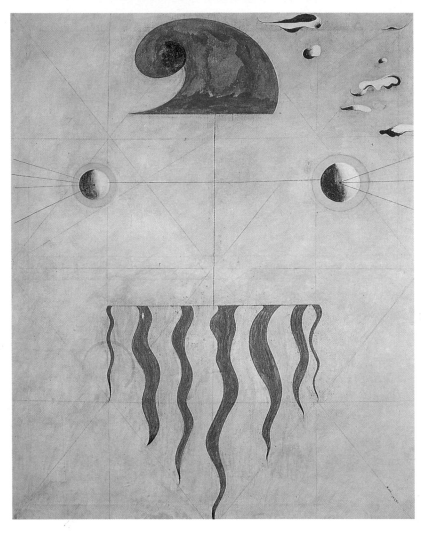

Left *Head of a Catalan Peasant* by Joan Miró. The peasant's red cap and his beard are set in a faint grid pattern that reminds us of the flat surface of the canvas. One eye is smaller than the other, so we can view the face as if it was turning to one side, while the clouds suggest a deep space with the 'eyes' as planets. (Private collection.)

Freud and the unconscious

The writers and artists known as Surrealists were interested in the researches of the psychiatrist, Sigmund Freud (1856–1939), who suggested that we are only conscious of a small part of the human mind. The rest, hidden below the surface like an iceberg, he called the Unconscious. We can only get a glimpse of this hidden world when our conscious mind is not working, for instance when we are asleep (in our dreams) or not concentrating, or when some accidental pattern in the world around us suddenly suggests an image.

Most of the post-war artists and designers discussed in the last chapter were trying to build a world where everything could be planned and organized sensibly and rationally. But there is another side to human beings – irrational, unplanned, unconscious. When you doodle in the margin of your book during a boring lesson what are you thinking about? Is your drawing deliberate or does it seem to happen by itself? When you dream, where do the weird images and happenings come from?

Throughout history, different people have linked art and creativity to the less conscious

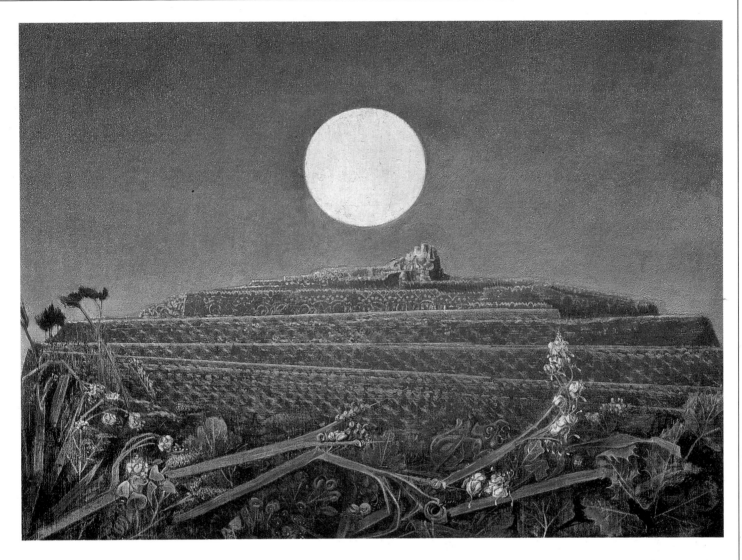

Right *The Entire City* by Max Ernst. Scraping wet paint across a canvas laid over different textures suggested an image which Ernst then developed into a haunting vision of an abandoned city. (Kunsthaus, Zurich.)

side of our minds. Leonardo da Vinci, in the fifteenth century, recommended that artists should encourage their imaginations by staring at the cracks and marks on walls. You may have seen 'faces' or other images in cloud formations, and perhaps you have found that drawings sometimes turn out better when you are not concentrating too hard.

The group of writers who, in 1924 first adopted the name Surrealism, was led by the poet André Breton (1896–1966). They experimented with what they called 'automatic writing'. They would try to go into a trance-like state so they could talk or write without really thinking about what they were saying. They also used to play a game like 'Consequences', in which each person would write a part of a sentence, then fold the paper to hide the words and pass it on to the next person to continue writing. They hoped the results of these experiments would suggest marvellous new images as well as revealing the workings of their subconscious minds.

Painters were excited by the new freedom Surrealism encouraged. The paintings by Joan Miró (1893–1983), sharp, bright pictures of his

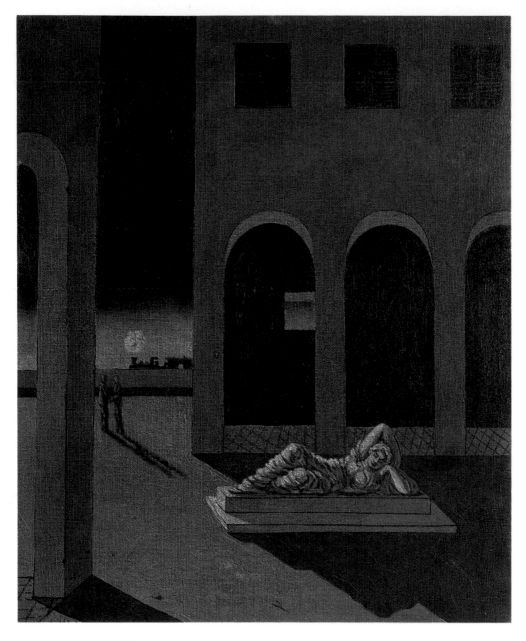

Italian Square – Melancholy by Georgio de Chirico. Long shadows and a suggestion of brooding silence give de Chirico's work a nightmare quality that was later copied in many Hollywood films. (Christies Gallery, London.)

family farm in Spain, became inhabited by fantastic creatures. He also experimented with a pictorial version of automatic writing, scrubbing paint thinly on to the canvas to suggest images. He wrote: 'As I paint, the picture begins to suggest itself under my brush. The form becomes a sign for a woman or a bird as I work. The first stage is free, unconscious. But the second stage is carefully calculated.'

Max Ernst (1891–1976) used a range of similar techniques. These included taking rubbings from heavily textured materials such as grained wood, with paper and crayon, or scraping paint away from canvas. Another Surrealist technique involved squeezing paint between two sheets of paper then peeling one sheet away. (You may have done this yourself with folded paper, which gives a symmetrical, butterfly-like image.)

Ernst also made collages using engraved illustrations cut from old catalogues, novels and magazines and put together in odd

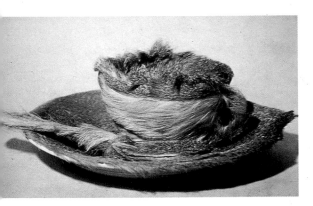

Above *Fur Breakfast* by Meret Oppenheim (b. 1913). Like other Surrealist works, this disturbing version of a familiar object was designed to upset normal expectations – the idea of using this cup and saucer makes us feel uneasy. (Museum of Modern Art, New York.)

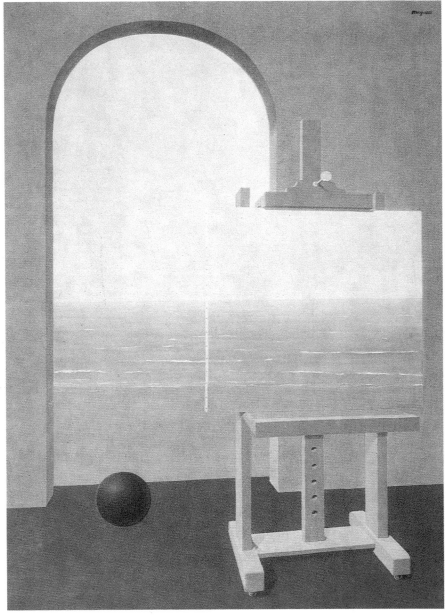

Right *The Human Condition* by René Magritte. Magritte made several versions of this theme, which reminds us that even the most convincing painted illusion is not real. Modern advertisements borrow many similar images from Surrealism, to catch our attention (Simon Spierer collection.)

combinations to produce mysterious or disturbing images, quite unlike the original Cubist use of the technique. A sculptural variation of this involved extraordinary mixes of objects, sometimes poetic, sometimes frightening or funny.

After the earlier period of automatic techniques in the 1920s, surrealist painting shifted towards the realistic depiction of dream-like scenes. The Italian artist, Giorgio de Chirico (1888–1978) had explored similar themes before the 1914 war, and his work was much admired by the Surrealists.

Other painters of these 'dream postcards' included Salvador Dali (1904–89), whose well-known pictures of soft watches are less Surrealist than the films he made with the film director Luis Buñuel. The paintings of the Belgian René Magritte (1898–1967) are more truly dream like, perhaps because they are of ordinary people, or places which just happen to have something odd about them.

9 REALISMS IN THE THIRTIES

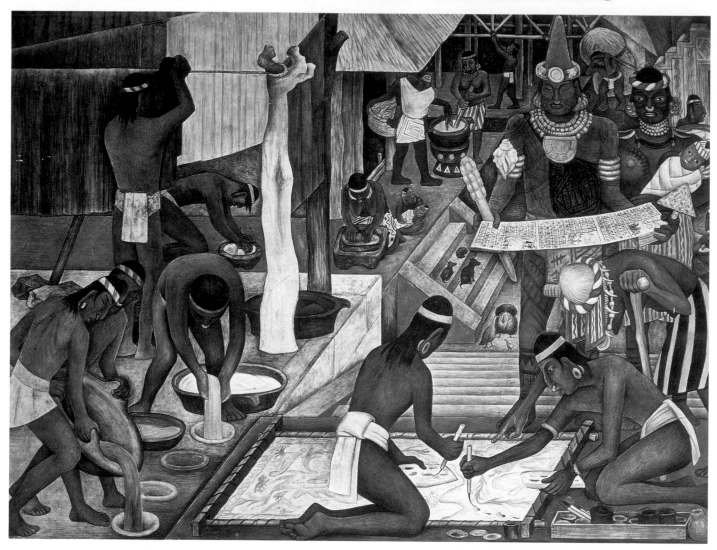

Tarasco Civilization – Fabric Dyeing by Diego Rivera. Rivera had been a Cubist painter in Paris. After his return to Mexico, he used a mixture of modern and traditional styles, in large wall paintings, telling the story of Mexican civilization. (National Palace, Mexico City.)

By the beginning of the 1930s, several groups of artists besides the Surrealists were reviving more conventional, realistic styles of painting, for many different reasons.

Traditional styles of representation do not usually draw attention to the artist's point of view, or how the image is constructed, so whatever is shown seems natural. In the 1930s, Hitler and Stalin, both political dictators, encouraged the use of this kind of realism for their official propaganda art, because it could make things seem true without people noticing that they were being persuaded.

Realism

'Realistic' is not quite such a straightforward word as it might at first seem to be. It is easier to think about what realistic means if we leave out the question of life-like drawing skills for the time being. Imagine you are going to take a photograph of a factory. You could stand a long way away so the factory seems to blend into its surroundings, or you could come in close so the building looms up against the sky. You could show the factory workers looking relaxed, or overworked, or proud of their achievements. If you are concerned about the environment, you might want to show pollution of local rivers, whereas the factory owners would probably choose a prettier view for their advertisements. Each of these photographs would be 'realistic' but they would show different aspects of reality. Have a look at some images and think about what decisions have been made.

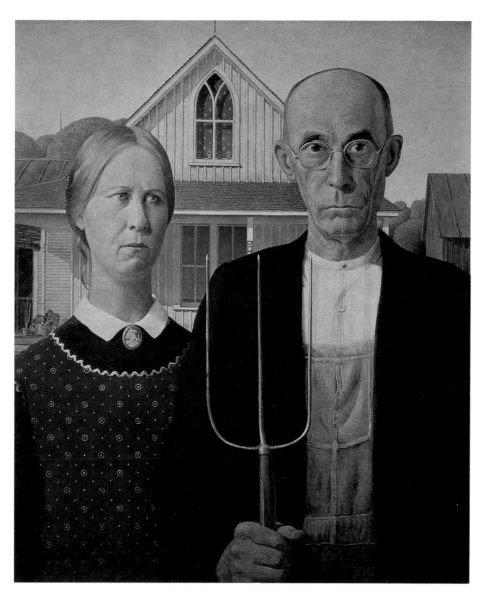

American Gothic by Grant Wood (1892–1942). It is easy to miss the careful staging of this famous image. At a time of terrible unemployment, Wood celebrated the values of rural small-town America in a dry, plain style that was part of his message. (Art Institute of Chicago.)

People who wanted to fight this kind of propaganda argued fiercely about the best way to do it. Some wanted to use the old familiar styles because they were popular. Others felt that because life was changing, old techniques of spreading information could not represent reality truthfully.

The German playwright Bertolt Brecht (1898–1956) believed that artists and writers should not use the same tricks, even in a good cause. Instead, they should help the audience to think for themselves by deliberately using techniques that would remind them that they are seeing something artificial. He said, 'I do

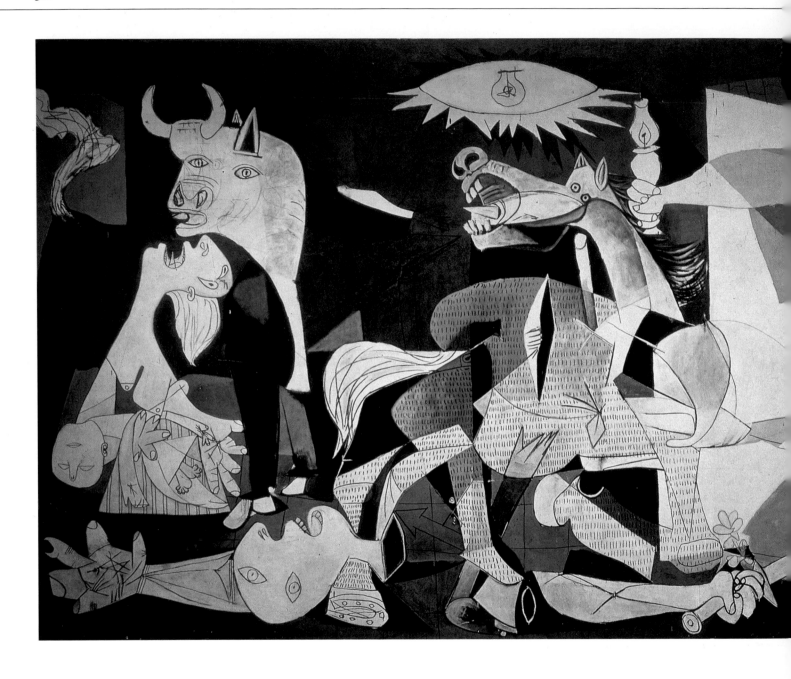

not want members of the audience to hang their brains up with their overcoats.'

But whatever the original intentions of modern art, the fact was that a lot of people still found it pointless or hard to understand. The world was in the middle of an economic depression with millions of people jobless and hungry; events in Europe were heading towards war again. Some artists began to wonder whether they should abandon the new ways of working, and deal with these big human issues in a more straightforward way.

In Mexico, Diego Rivera (1886–1957), José Oroszco (1883–1949) and David Siqueiros (1896–1974) were helping to establish a new democratic regime, telling the story of the

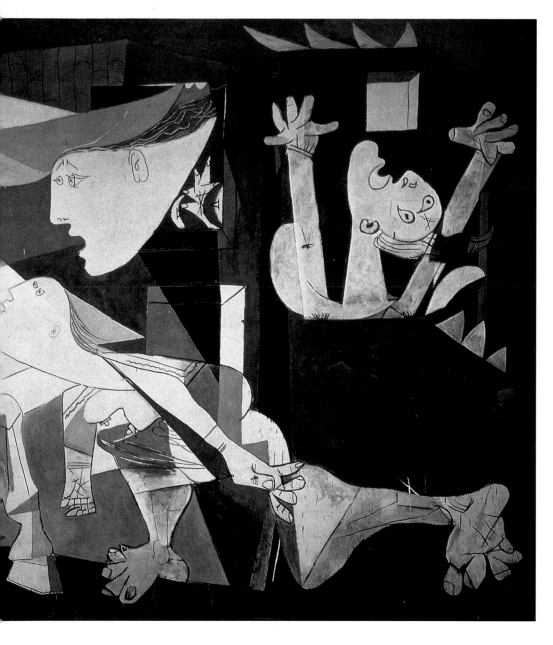

Guernica by Pablo Picasso. This huge mural was painted after the town of Guernica was destroyed by German bombers supporting General Franco's Fascist army during the Spanish Civil War (1936–39). It was the first time that air power had been used to kill civilians including women and children. The painting was displayed in the Spanish Pavilion at the Paris World Fair in 1937, just two months after the bombing. Picasso used no colour, just black, white and grey (perhaps to remind us of newsprint) and he also included echoes of several earlier war paintings. Although some people felt that a more 'realistic' style was needed to help influence public opinion over this atrocity, the work had a huge impact. (Prado, Madrid.)

Mexican people in massive wall paintings (see page 30). These combined elements of the ancient Aztec and Mayan civilizations with other styles, including Roman frescoes and Renaissance figure paintings as well as modern art. Another Mexican artist, Frida Kahlo (1907–54) drew on traditional styles for more personal work which was greatly admired by the European surrealists.

In the USA (as part of the 'New Deal' to help the unemployed), many artists were commissioned to paint public murals. Many of them used the example of the Mexican artists to develop a popular, realistic style. There was also a deliberate move away from modern European styles in favour of plain, 'no-nonsense' paintings celebrating a rural American life-style.

10 ABSTRACT EXPRESSIONISM

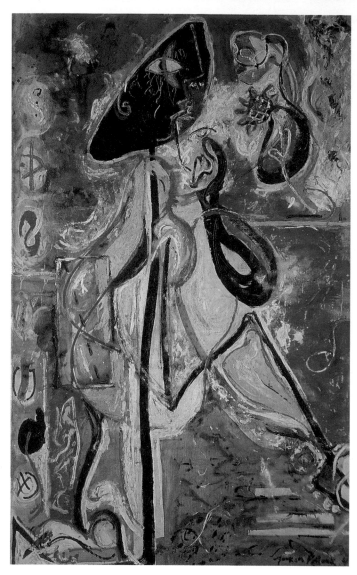

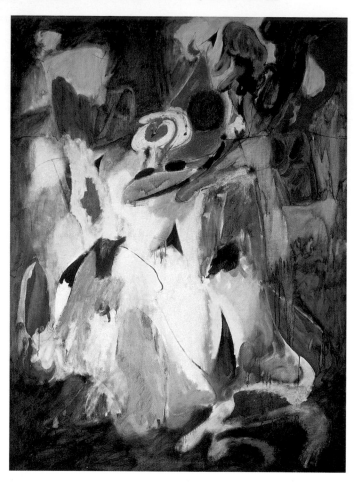

Left *Moon Woman* by Jackson Pollock. The title refers to a native American legend, but the rhythmic pattern of the paint is as important as the image. In his most famous works, Pollock laid the canvas on the floor and dripped the paint in delicate webs of colour. (Museum of Modern Art, New York.)

Painters and sculptors can work almost anywhere. But they also need to be where they can discuss their work with other artists, get it shown and talked about, and find people to buy it. In this century, most major cities have had some kind of network of galleries, collectors and critics. Just as Hollywood has become the centre of the film industry, Paris was the centre of the professional art world until the Second World War (1939–45). Many artists and dealers then left Europe for the

USA, and attention gradually shifted to New York.

At this time, most younger American artists were influenced by Europeans like Picasso, Matisse, Miró and Léger, whose work they knew through magazines and exhibitions. Many of them had been involved with public art projects, which had helped to give them some professional confidence. Like other artists at that time, they felt that art should deal

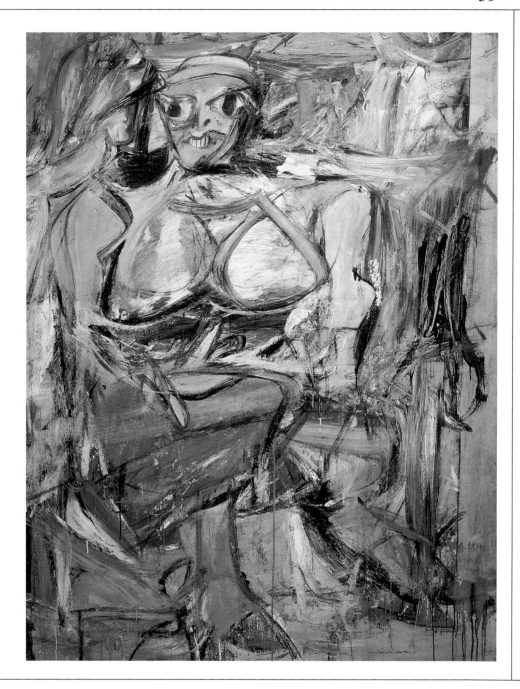

Left *Waterfall* by Arshile Gorky. Gorky's late work combined a very physical use of paint with delicate line drawings, derived from landscape or human figures. (Tate Gallery, London.)

Right *Woman I*, by Willem de Kooning. De Kooning's abstract work of the 1940s developed from drawings of the human figure, cut up and overlaid with heavy, apparently random paint marks. His *Woman* series brings back the whole figure, but with savage humour. (Museum of Modern Art, New York.)

with human subject matter, and that purely geometric abstract art had become cold and empty without the idealism of Mondrian's generation.

Picasso's *Guernica* (see pages 32–3) offered a different kind of model, and several of the Americans were painting works with partly abstract figures in a shallow, Cubist-type space. Surrealist ideas about the unconscious mind encouraged Arshile Gorky (1904–48) to draw

on memories of his childhood in Armenia, in a series of loose, almost doodling paintings.

During the 1940s, artists began to take more interest in the actual process of painting. There was a widespread interest in the notion that, like handwriting, the kind of marks you make with paint can show your state of mind. Some artists also compared the act of painting to the rituals of certain native American tribes, such as the sand paintings of the Navaho Indians.

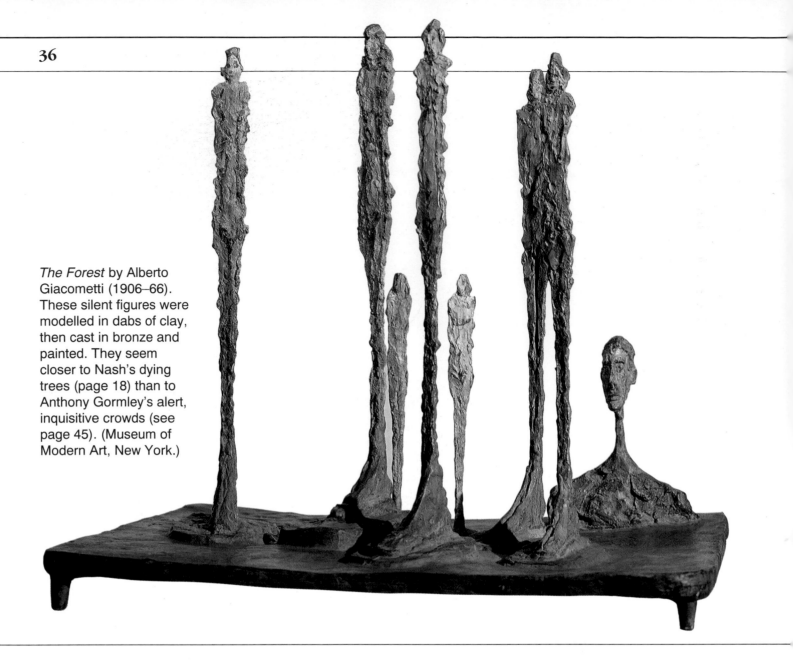

The Forest by Alberto Giacometti (1906–66). These silent figures were modelled in dabs of clay, then cast in bronze and painted. They seem closer to Nash's dying trees (page 18) than to Anthony Gormley's alert, inquisitive crowds (see page 45). (Museum of Modern Art, New York.)

Critics often emphasized the unplanned and energetic way that paintings were made, and pointed out similarities to the way that jazz musicians use improvisation.

A group of New York painters, including Jackson Pollock (1912–56), Barnett Newman (1905–70), the Dutchman Willem de Kooning 1904–89), and Russian-born Mark Rothko (1903–70), became known as the Abstract Expressionists. Their paintings look very different from each other, but they shared certain beliefs about what art should be.

After the explosion of the first atomic bomb in 1945, at the end of the Second World War,

human life could seem, to a great many people, pretty small and insignificant in the face of a huge empty universe. Any form of self-expression was a heroic act of defiance – an insistence that human beings do matter. In Europe after the war, a similar mood was often expressed through paintings or sculptures of the human figure, but the Abstract Expressionists believed that an abstract (but not impersonal) art could reach deeper levels of feeling.

The wish to turn personal feelings into grand statements may be one reason why they began to make paintings much larger than before. Looking at tiny reproductions in a book like

Red on Maroon by Mark Rothko. Photographs cannot convey the impact of Rothko's works and the subtle way the colours smoulder against each other. In real life, they are like giant doorways floating in space, pulling the spectator into their 'magnetic' field. Rothko had been involved in experimental theatre and wanted his paintings to work like abstract dramas, drawing us in emotionally and physically. (Tate Gallery, London.)

this, it is easy to forget what an impact really big paintings can have.

When a painting is taller than you are, and stretches sideways, wider than you can see in one glance, it changes the way you look at it. Rather than looking into the picture, as if through a window frame, the larger picture makes you explore it just as you might explore the room you are standing in. You become much more involved in the painting. Many paintings by Jackson Pollock and Barnett Newman have this effect, which you can also feel with the Impressionist pictures of water lilies painted many years earlier by Claude Monet (1840–1926).

When they were younger, these New York artists had felt like outsiders. All the important living artists seemed to be on the other side of the Atlantic, and at home, modern art was sneered at as a dangerous, possibly Communist, foreign invention. Very soon after the war, however, they began to achieve some success. By the middle of the 1950s, New York had become the centre of the art world, and the US government was sending exhibitions of their work around the world as a display of American freedom. Abstract Expressionism had become the official art, and all the heroic talk was beginning to sound rather overblown to a new generation. It was time for something different.

11 POP ART AND THE SIXTIES

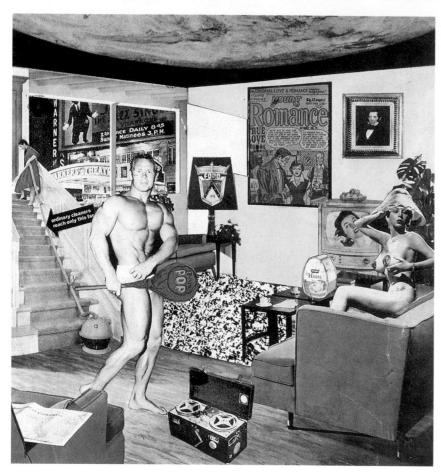

Just what is it that makes today's homes so different, so appealing? by Richard Hamilton. This little collage is made from advertisements for the new consumer goods and popular entertainments of the 1950s. The muscleman's lollipop helped to give Pop Art its name. (Collection of Edwin Janss Jr, California.)

For more than a hundred years, the way that art is displayed and discussed has tended to take it away from everyday life and into museums, encouraging the idea that people need special knowledge to understand and appreciate it. Some people have welcomed this separateness because it could give artists more freedom to experiment.

Others have tried to make art connect with our daily lives by including images from so-called popular culture – the cheap and cheerful things that usually get left out of official views of 'serious' art. Post-Impressionist pictures of circuses and Cubist newspaper collages are examples – but they now hang respectably in museums.

In the 1950s, British artists, brought up in a grey post-war world, had a rather romantic view of American popular culture – Hollywood films, rock'n'roll music and glamorous, glossy cars. In 1956, a group of them organized an exhibition called 'This is Tomorrow'. The artist, Richard Hamilton (b. 1922), whose collage (shown above) helped to give Pop Art its name, argued that modern art should not be pompous, but young, witty and fun. This view was shared by a number of younger artists, including Peter Blake (b. 1932) and David Hockney (b. 1937), at that time students at the Royal College of Art, in London.

American artists had a slightly different attitude. Claes Oldenburg (b. 1929) celebrated

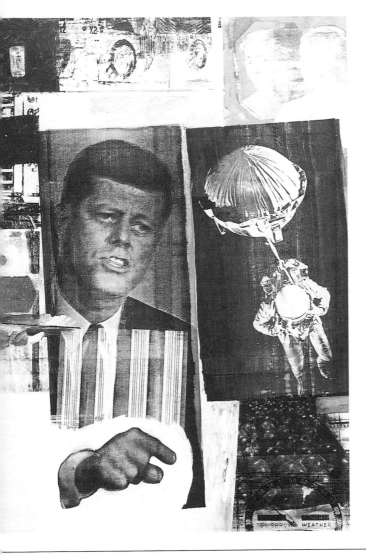

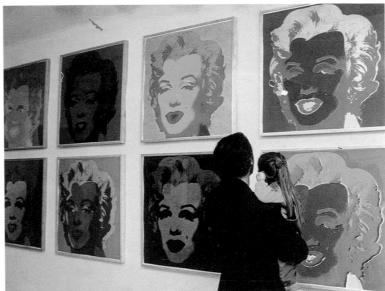

Left *Retroactive II* by Robert Rauschenberg. New printing techniques enabled Rauschenberg to mix newspaper images, reproductions of famous paintings and hand-painted areas of colour. (Collection of Stefan T. Edlis.)

Above *Marilyn Monroe* by Andy Warhol. Warhol's images of the Hollywood star explore the fascination of fame and the way that repetition eventually leaves us feeling bored. (Viewed during the inauguration of the Warhol system, Paris 1990.)

the sheer messiness of New York street life. Jasper Johns (b. 1930) produced images of the American flag with heavily worked, almost expressionist, paint surfaces, while his colleague Robert Rauschenberg (b. 1925) used photography and silk-screen printing to make densely-layered images that resemble Dada collages.

Many other American Pop artists preferred the impersonal feel of advertising and other mass-produced imagery. After all the emotional language used about Abstract Expressionism, the younger generation wanted to be 'cool' and impassive. Instead of expressing inner feelings or observations from nature, they made second-hand images – pictures of

pictures. Roy Lichtenstein (b. 1923) copied the machine-printed look of comic strips, while Andy Warhol (1928–87) took news photos or pictures of soup cans or film stars, and repeated them over and over again. This apparently mindless repetition prompted questions about Warhol's intentions. Was he making a point about the way that newspapers and TV bombard us with images so relentlessly that we stop thinking about what they mean? Why should the meaning of a work depend on knowing what the artist thought? Was the whole point of the work to make us think about these kinds of questions?

These are complicated issues, but Pop Art appealed to people for its easily recognized

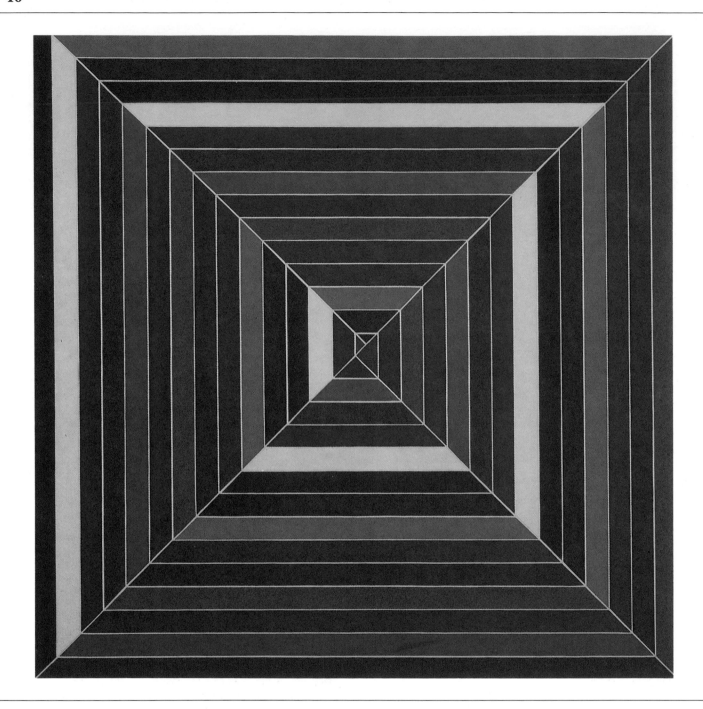

subject-matter and its bright colours, which seemed to echo what was happening in fashion and pop music as well.

The idea that teenagers were a special group with their own tastes in clothes and music really began in the mid–1950s, with cinema idols like James Dean and rock stars like Elvis Presley. By the early 1960s, youth culture meant mini skirts and the Beatles. A lot of the new art, like fashion and advertising, was bright and brash and shiny.

Several American and British sculptors, like David Smith (1906–65) and Anthony Caro (b. 1924) were making large pieces, in polished or painted metal, that seemed to make few references to natural forms. Others were exploiting the possibilities of new materials such as fibreglass and plastic.

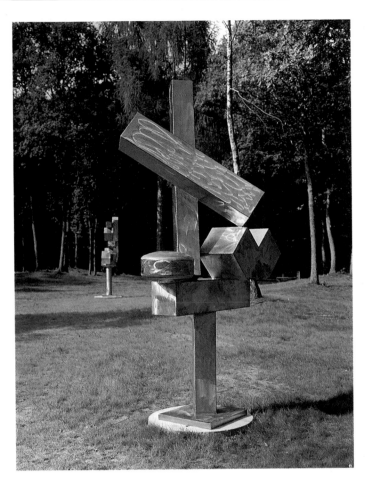

Above *Cubi XVIII* by David Smith. Smith ground his steel surfaces to catch the light, so that the solid volumes seem to balance almost weightlessly in the sunshine. (Private Collection.)

Left *Hyena Stomp* by Frank Stella. A simple geometric pattern, taller than a man, produces unexpected illusions of space. Stella later produced relief sculptures which push exuberantly off the wall and back into real space. (Tate Gallery, London.)

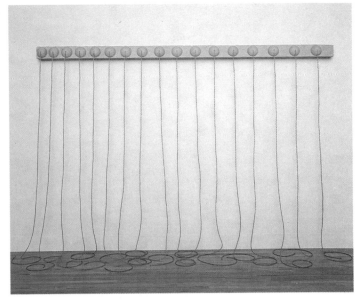

Above *Addendum* by American artist Eva Hesse. The logical, repetitive structures of Minimal art (see below) become illogical and absurd in Hesse's work. Here the mathematical spacing of the grey domes is undermined by the rubber tubing which droops randomly on to the floor. (Tate Gallery, London.)

American Frank Stella (b. 1936) was one of several painters making pictures which seemed to be about nothing other than themselves – repeated patterns painted in metallic or synthetic colours. He refused to let people read any kind of expressionist meaning into these works, saying 'What you see is what you see'. The taste for simplicity and repetition was shared by those artists (mainly sculptors) whose work was known as Minimal Art.

Minimal Art
Minimal Art was the name given to work which used very simple shapes often repeated. Whereas earlier twentieth-century sculpture was often intended to be seen out of doors, Minimal sculpture usually needed to be seen in a gallery space. Its critics claimed that if it wasn't shown in a gallery, you would never guess that it was supposed to be art. In fact, these works often have a very powerful presence in real life, however boring they may seem in photographs. As the sculptor Robert Morris (b. 1931) said, 'simple shapes don't necessarily produce a simple experience.' It is rather like listening to music with a strong, simple beat. Sharing the enclosed space of a gallery with these orderly structures draws attention to the difference between the way we perceive things with our bodies and with our minds. As we move around them, the pattern we know stays the same while the pattern we see is constantly changing.

12 THE LAST TWENTY-FIVE YEARS

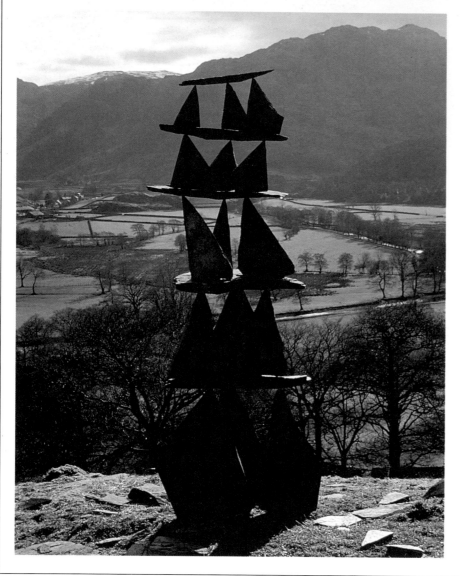

Left *Balanced Slates* by British sculptor Andy Goldsworthy (b. 1956). Goldsworthy is interested in movement, change, growth and decay, and has worked with materials as fragile and shortlived as leaves and snow. Here, in the Lake District of England, a temporary balance has been achieved.

Over the last quarter of a century, many artists have challenged the idea (strongly argued by several critics in the 1960s) that art should be a specialist activity, to be judged only on its own terms – painting, for instance, only being 'about' colour and flatness and shape. Although this view produced some powerful work (just as scientific progress often comes from people exploring ideas for their own sake rather than to solve specific problems), it also led to much undemanding and tasteful art, as bland as background music.

During the 1960s, many artists were involved in the Civil Rights Movement, the Women's Movement and in protests against the Vietnam War. They began to find that the 'pure' view of art was being used as an excuse to ignore any work which raised these uncomfortable issues. In particular, many black and women artists wanted to make art which described their own experiences, and to explore the ways that images (in advertising, for instance) encourage very limited stereotyped views of different groups of people.

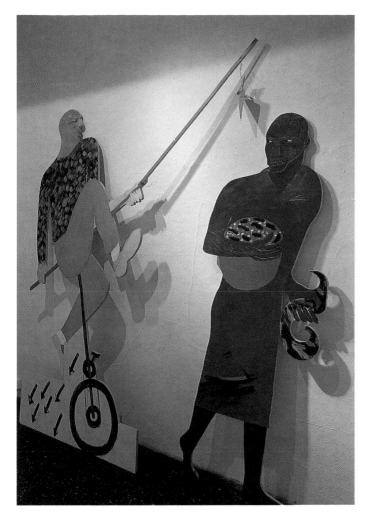

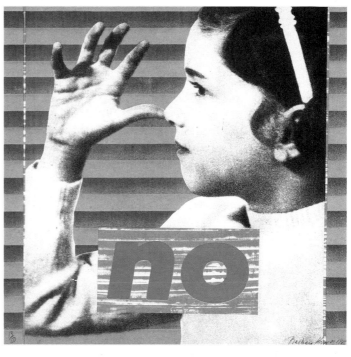

Above *Untitled*, by American artist Barbara Kruger (b. 1945). Like Himid, Kruger uses humour to undermine accepted images, mixing photographs and captions in the glossy styles of magazines and posters. (Tate Gallery, London.)

Above *The Carrot Piece* by Lubaina Himid, who was born in Tanzania in 1954. She has described her work as 'a mixture of humour, fury, celebration and optimism. . . . I want to destroy the stereotypes that television, the newspapers and advertisements are constantly feeding us . . . (and show) black women as independent, strong-thinking people.' (Private collection.)

There have been different ideas about what form such work should take. Some artists have felt the need to return to more traditional styles of painting or sculpture to reach a wider audience. Others believe that these complicated and important subjects need the widest possible range of approaches. These have included photography, writing, video and performance art – in addition to the richness and freedom of expression that painting and sculpture have acquired in the last hundred years.

During the late 1960s, some Minimal artists began to explore looser structures, where the making process was more important than the final shape, which was often a matter of chance. Using soft material, sewn or stacked or hanging, artists like Eva Hesse (1936–70) produced works that were sometimes squashy, humorous echoes of the human body, and sometimes more mysterious (see page 41).

The interest in process and unusual materials also took the form of so-called Earth Art, in

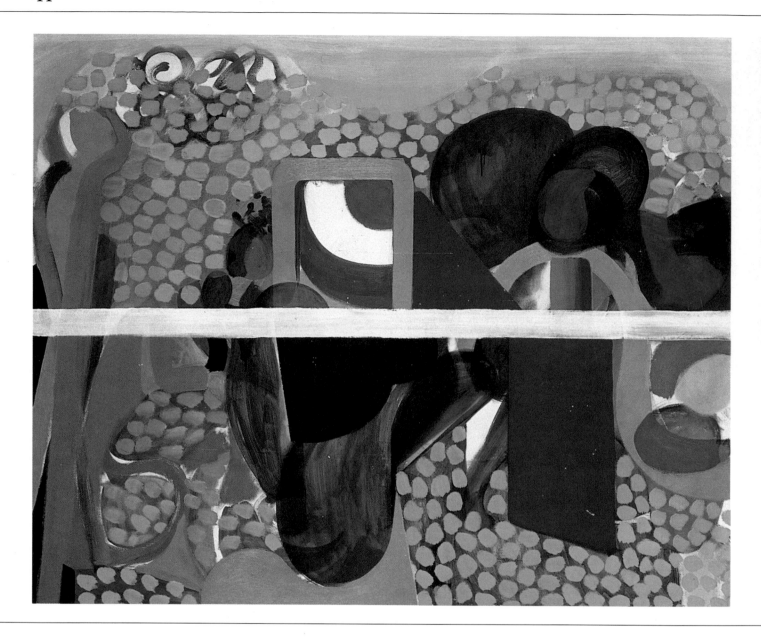

which artists used the landscape itself as their material. This coincided with the beginning of the environmental movement and a growing concern for the future of the natural world. However, many projects involved considerable interference with nature, such as *Spiral Jetty* by the American Robert Smithson (1938–73), or the work of Bulgarian-born Christo (b. 1935) who wrapped whole areas of coastline in cloth. Other work, such as that of Britain's Richard Long (b. 1945), was gentler. Because much of this work was temporary or sited in remote areas, most people only knew it through photographs and descriptions. It was often the idea of the work that captured their imaginations.

Ideas, also communicated through photographs and writings, were the main point of Conceptual art. Many Conceptual artists were influenced by the work of Marcel Duchamp (see page 19) and his attempts to prod people into questioning the things they took for granted. The German artist Joseph Beuys (1921–86) also had an enormous influence on younger artists, with work that cut across many different categories – lectures, performance, sculpture and installations.

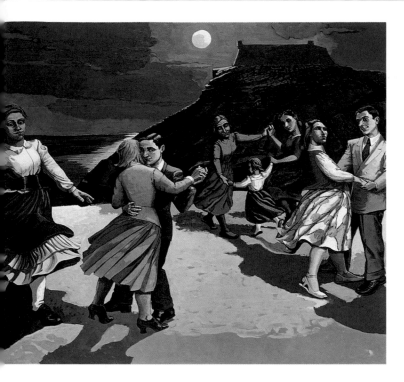

Above *The Dance* by Portuguese-born Paula Rego (b. 1935). Why are these solid figures dancing in the moonlight? The shadows they cast are not consistent, increasing the sense of mystery in this oddly tender scene. (Tate Gallery, London.)

Left *Dinner at West Hill* by the English artist Howard Hodgkin (b. 1932). Hodgkin's pleasure in the brilliant colour and pattern of Indian miniature painting is evident in this early example of his work. (Tate Gallery, London.)

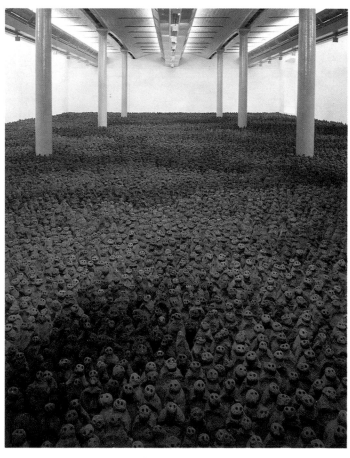

Above *Field for the British Isles* by Britain's Anthony Gormley (b. 1950). Children from a local school worked with Gormley to produce the 40,000 little figures that crowd this room, staring up at the spectator. (Tate Gallery, Liverpool.)

His passionate belief that art has a social and political purpose was shared by many people.

The 1980s also saw plenty of revivals or parodies of earlier work, in art as well as fashion, films and television. Some people have taken this as proof that our age has no original ideas of its own, but playing games with the past is one way of moving forward from it.

In spite of new technologies and all the alternative types of art, painting and sculpture have survived – figurative as well as abstract, expressionistic as well as 'cool'.

The exciting thing about the art being made right now is that people have not had time to create theories about it, or to try to tell you what is important. You have to make up your own mind about what you like, just as you choose what music to listen to. Many young artists now are concerned about the same sort of things as you – bodies and feelings, how we relate to each other and how we fit into the world. Whenever you get a chance to visit art galleries, try to go with an open mind (and perhaps a friend to share ideas with). But above all, have the confidence to use your eyes and trust your judgement.

GLOSSARY

Abstract The description of a painting that explores shapes, colours and textures and shows them as satisfying in their own right, not as ways of depicting the real world.

Academies Official schools where painters and sculptors were trained. By the nineteenth century these schools insisted on a style based on past art, and so 'academic' has come to mean a rather fixed and old fashioned approach to art.

Art Deco A style of decoration, jewellery, architecture etc. (abbreviated from the 1925 Exhibition of Decorative Art). The style was at its height in the 1930s.

Automatic Something done without conscious thought, like doodling.

Caricature An image of a person which exaggerates the person's features.

Classical Following the ideas originally expressed in the arts of ancient Greece and Rome which emphasized simplicity, balance and beauty.

Commissioned When an artist is asked to produce a work of art for a particular purpose or customer.

Communist Following the political ideas of Communism which state that everyone should be equal and share in the wealth created by industry.

Composition The arrangement of the various parts of a work such as a painting or piece of music.

Construction A piece of sculpture made by joining separate parts together (such as by nailing or welding) rather than carving into wood or stone, or modelling in a soft material like plaster or clay.

Depression A long period of economic difficulty and unemployment (especially the period between 1929 and 1934 in the USA and Europe).

Fascism A system of government which controls everything in a country and which suppresses all public criticism or opposition.

Figurative Relating to the natural representation of things.

Functional Designed to be practical and useful rather than decorative.

Iberian Relating to the pre-Roman peoples of the Iberian peninsula (Spain and Portugal).

Impressionist The name given to a group of painters working in the latter half of the nineteenth century, who concentrated on recording the effects of light and colour.

Installation A work of art, like a huge sculpture, through which spectators move.

Medium (plural: media) The material used in a work of art.

Murals Large paintings on walls.

Nationalism Pride in one's country, sometimes to the exclusion of other people.

'New Deal' A government programme in the USA in the mid-1930s designed to get people back into work and end the Depression.

Parodies Works of art that mimic the style of others in a humorous way.

Performance art A work of art that is actually carried out in front of the audience, often in the form of a series of actions performed by the artist.

Perspective A system to enable artists to represent objects and space on a flat surface.

Popular culture The objects and art forms that are used by the majority of people, rather than the more specialized forms of art.

Propaganda A campaign of publicity which aims to persuade people to believe certain things or think in certain ways.

Rational Describing beliefs or ideas which are based on thought rather than on emotions or feelings.

'Ready-mades' A term used by Marcel Duchamp and others to describe ordinary objects (not chosen for their beauty) altered slightly and exhibited as if they were works of art.

Realistic In art, the effort to make a work of art represent the world as we see it.

Relief A work of art made in three dimensions, like sculpture, but designed to be set against a flat surface such as a wall and viewed from one side, like a painting.

Rubbings Images of objects with raised patterns or textures, such as coins or tree bark, which are taken by rubbing a crayon across a sheet of paper on top of the object.

Salon In France, an annual government-sponsored exhibition of art.

Spiritual Concerned with deeper or more religious aspects of life rather than physical or material things.

Stereotype A description which gives the same characteristics to a whole group of people, which denies them any individual qualities.

Still-life A painting or drawing of inanimate objects, such as flowers, fruit, books etc.

Symbolic Using images or elements such as colour to represent something else (such as an idea or feeling which cannot be shown directly).

Symbolists Artists painting at the end of the nineteenth century who incorporated symbolic meanings in their work.

Women's Movement The campaign (particularly in the 1960s and '70s) to change the law (and people's attitudes) to bring about the achievement of equal rights for women.

FURTHER READING

Bohm-Duchen, Monica *Understanding Modern Art* (Usborne, 1993).

Cole, Alison *Perspective* (Dorling Kindersley, 1992).

Davidson, Rosemary *What is Art?* (Oxford Books, 1993).

Powell, Jillian *Twentieth Century Art* (Wayland, 1990).

Richardson, Wendy and Jack *The World of Art series* (Macmillan, 1989-91).

For older readers

Chadwick, Whitney *Women, Art and Society* (Thames and Hudson, 1990).

Hughes, Robert *The Shock of the New* (Thames and Hudson, 1991).

Lynton, Norbert *Modern Art* (Phaidon, reprinted 1990).

Stangos, Nikos (ed.) *Concepts of Modern Art* (Thames and Hudson, 1993).

WHERE TO SEE MODERN ART

In London, the National Gallery has some early twentieth-century work; the Tate Gallery has the main public collection of modern art, and the Saatchi Collection also has important examples. The Hayward, Whitechapel and Serpentine Galleries hold temporary exhibitions, as do many of the small commercial galleries. Most of the other major cities in Britain have permanent and special exhibitions in their museums and galleries. Many museums arrange special activities for children during the school holidays and these can be a fun way to get to know new work.

In Paris, the Musée Nationale d'Art Moderne and the Centre Georges Pompidou have permanent and special exhibitions. The Musée Picasso, also in Paris, has an excellent collection of work by this artist. Most large European cities have museums of modern art, including the Rijksmuseum Kroller-Muller at Otterlo and Amsterdam Stedlijk in the Netherlands, The Munich Neue Pinakothek and the Stuttgart Staatsgalerie in Germany.

Because many of the early collectors of modern art were American, the United States has particularly fine collections, including the Museum of Modern Art, the Guggenheim Museum and the Whitney Museum of Modern Art in New York and San Francisco Museum of Modern art.

The publishers would like to point out that where there are variations in spelling or definition regarding the artists and works in this book, the example of *The Penguin Dictionary of Art and Artists*, reprinted in 1991, has been followed.

INDEX

Numbers in **bold** refer to illustrations